THE BACKYARD HARVEST

50 CONTAINER GARDENING PROJECTS

TO GROW
FOOD, FLOWERS AND MORE
ALL YEAR LONG

SUSAN PATTERSON
Master Gardener

BACKYARD
·VITALITY·

C O N T E N T S

THE JOY OF CREATIVE CONTAINER GARDENING

> "Half the interest of a garden is the constant exercise of the imagination."
>
> — C.W. Earle, *Pot-Pourri From A Surrey Garden*, 1897

Container gardening is so much fun. Not only do containers make gardening a possibility for everyone, even those with little space, but they also make great decor pieces. A creative container garden is like a work of art.

You would not believe how many conversations have been started over unique containers that I have planted over the years. It is so exciting to see the expression on people's faces when they encounter strange objects in my garden housing beautiful flowers or flourishing vegetables, herbs, or fruit. Their usual comment is, "I didn't know that you could do that." To which my response is simply, "If it holds soil, and drains well, you can do it!"

Containers of all kinds look great scattered throughout your garden or as a focal point on decks, porches, patios, or in any outdoor living space. I always enjoy finding new and interesting ways to plant flowers, herbs, veggies, and even fruit.

Some of my best and most imaginative containers have been the ones I have found alongside the road, at thrift stores, yard sales, and even in people's trash! You know what they say, "One man's trash is another man's treasure!" To me it is, "One man's trash is another happy home for a plant and one less item in a landfill."

Container food gardening is quite popular, especially for people who have limited space. Containers are so flexible, you can move them or hang them anywhere. You will be amazed at how many possible planting containers you throw away daily and how much landfill debris you can save by using recycled options.

I am excited to share with you fifty of my favorite imaginative container garden ideas that are environmentally friendly and lots of fun to make.

Ready to get your hands dirty?

Susan Patterson, Master Gardener

. . . .

This book is dedicated to my creative
and industrious husband Thomas who is always
getting his hands dirty!

. . . .

GROWING FLOWERS IN CONTAINERS

"Flowers don't worry about how they're going to bloom. They just open up and turn toward the light and that makes them beautiful." — Jim Carrey

I look forward to planting my container flowers every year. It is always exciting to find new and interesting ways to display flowers on my deck, porch and in outdoor living spaces. Here are some tips for growing beautiful flower containers all season long.

Drainage, Drainage, Drainage

First and foremost don't ever plant a flower in a container without considering drainage. Strangely, I have even bought container plants at the store only to find out they don't have any drainage at all. Without drainage, the roots of plants become too wet and this causes the plant to die. The best size for drainage holes is ½ inch for a medium planter and 1 inch for a large container.

Learn The Light

Evaluate how much light you have in the areas where you want to position your containers. There are so many different plants to choose from, some that like low light, some that like full shade, partial sun and those that do best in full sun. They key is to know your plants, group them together according to their light requirements, and position them in the right place.

Keep The Tags

Reading and keeping the tags that come with your plants is especially important if you are new to gardening. I recommend that you keep a plant journal to make note of what you planted where and with what other plants. This helps you remember what worked well and what did not do so well for future years. Plant tags will give you all of the information you need to know to care for plants.

Acclimation Is Critical

A lot of plants respond poorly to abrupt changes in temperature or amount of light. Always allow a few days to a week for your plants to get used to the climate at your home before planting them. Don't forget to water them during this time.

Soil Matters

When planting flowers in containers, be sure to use high-quality, lightweight soil—and plenty of it! Even if you use a large container, don't be tempted to fill the bottom half with junk. The more soil you put in, the better water retention and healthier roots you'll have.

Maintenance Counts

If you have a "plant it and forget it" mentality with container gardening, you will be disappointed. In many respects, container gardening requires more work than conventional gardening. Three musts with container gardening are pinching, pruning, and watering. Pinching and pruning after plants have flowered will encourage healthy growth and blooms. Extra special attention needs to be given to each container with an appropriate amount of water. The payoff for this extra effort will amaze you and make your container flower gardens spectacular!

Plant Shopping

Going for half-dead, discounted plants might be good on your wallet but they won't do much for your container aesthetics. Shop for healthy plants with good color and bright foliage. Sickly plants are more susceptible to transplant shock and may or may not make it once planted.

Feeding Hungry Plants

To keep both annuals and perennials looking their best, provide regular feeding throughout the gardening season. For best results, use an all-purpose organic feed for plants and flowers.

Mulching

Adding mulch to your containers is a great way to keep roots cool and retain moisture. It also adds a nice decorative touch to container arrangements. It is best to add a lightweight mulch that will allow good airflow.

Remove And Replace

Container flower gardens can start to get a little tired by the middle of the growing season. Don't be afraid to pull out plants and replace them with fresh ones. Perennials can be cut back and planted in your garden and will bloom again the following season.

Pre-Winter

Once a hard frost hits, your annuals will die. Throw those into your compost pile and plant any perennials for next year. Be sure to discard your soil into your compost pile as well and clean your containers for next year.

A Note About Perennials

Perennial plants are those that come back each year. Select perennials that are appropriate for your growing region. Generally speaking, your local greenhouse or plant supply store will only carry plants appropriate for your region. Perennials add a great deal of interest to pots and can form the anchor or focal point around which you can plant seasonal flowers.

If you wish to overwinter the perennial in a pot, choose a plant that is cold hardy to two USDA zones lower than the one you are in. Be sure to mulch perennials well and place them in an unheated garage or shed. Don't forget to provide water a few weeks before the first hard frost and again a few weeks before the spring growing season.

Treasure Trunk

Opening up old trunks is a passion of mine. It's not that I am looking for a treasure trove; it's the thought of releasing all sorts of memories unknown that intrigues me. Who used this trunk to keep their treasures? Did someone sail to a far-away spot with their entire life stored within the trunk? Did a young lady use it as her hope chest, for her fine linens, candles, and cookware as she prepared for marriage to her Prince Charming?

At any rate, old trunks are awesome, not to mention that they provide a spectacular place to display fine flowers or grow veggies, herbs, and fruit. Ready to make your old trunk come alive?

WHAT YOU NEED

- Old trunk of any shape or size
- Scissors
- Drill
- 1/2" drill bit
- Lightweight plastic tote that will fit inside the trunk
- Smaller lightweight plastic tote that will fit inside the above tote
- Pea gravel
- Lightweight potting mix
- Plants

HOW TO MAKE IT

1. Place your trunk planter where you want it in your garden. It will be harder to move once planted.

2. Put two inches of pea gravel in the bottom of the trunk.

3. Place the larger tote inside the trunk. Mark a cut line so that the tote is one inch below the sides of the trunk.

4. Place the smaller tote inside the larger tote. Mark a cut line so that the top edge of the tote is one inch from the top edge of the larger tote.

5. Remove the totes from the trunk.

6. Drill drainage holes in the bottom and sides (near the bottom) of both totes.

7. Place three inches of pea gravel inside the smaller tote.

8. Fill the smaller tote a little more than halfway with potting mix.

9. Place your plants in the trunk.

10. Finish filling up your trunk with potting mix and top with mulch.

11. Water well.

TIP: If your trunk is large, place a taller plant in the center surrounded by smaller plants and some vines for a beautiful cascading effect.

Beautiful Boot Bouquet

There comes a time in the life of every cherished pair of boots where although they have served you well in their years adorning your feet, you must bid farewell to your faithful friends. When this day arrives, don't just callously toss your hole-riddled, cracked soled shoes in the trash...make them useful once again!

Remember, with container gardening, creativity is key. The sky's the limit. Embrace your inner old-Western cowboy and class up your yard with some floral footwear.

- ❑ Pair of old boots
- ❑ Drill and 1/2" drill bit
- ❑ Lightweight potting mix
- ❑ Plants
- ❑ Mulch

HOW TO MAKE IT

1. Remove insoles from boots.
2. Drill at least five drainage holes, one inch apart, in the bottom and sides of each boot.
3. Fill your boots about halfway with lightweight potting soil.
4. Loosen roots on plants and place in boots.
5. Top with lightweight potting mix and mulch.
6. Water well.

TIP: Get creative! Place the boots on a welcome mat or on your front porch.

Tasteful Toolbox

Screwdrivers, hammers, and wrenches are important, but for the avid container gardener, old tool boxes can take on an even more vital purpose: beautifying your yard or patio. I love searching through yard sales, thrift stores, and my own garage to find shockingly empty boxes that still smell faintly of rust and filling them with soil and new life.

WHAT YOU NEED

- ❑ Old toolbox
- ❑ Drill
- ❑ 1/2" drill bit
  (if your toolbox still has its
  bottom intact)
- ❑ Lightweight potting mix
- ❑ Plants
- ❑ Mulch

HOW TO MAKE IT

1. Drill three drainage holes in each side of the toolbox and three on the bottom as well.

2. Fill the toolbox about halfway with lightweight potting mix.

3. Loosen roots on plants and place in toolbox.

4. Top with lightweight potting mix and mulch.

5. Water well.

TIP: Add some colored glass mulch to your toolbox for a real pop.

Tea Time

Ah, there is nothing quite like a warm cup of tea on a cold rainy day to warm the soul and cheer the spirit. Whether you prefer chamomile, chai, lemongrass, or plain old green tea, you are sure to find comfort in the first sip of a piping hot mug of your favorite brew. As you plant your flowers in your old tea kettle or teapot, reminisce on all the times you have enjoyed hearing the whistle of an awaiting kettle on the stove.

WHAT YOU NEED

- ❏ Old tea kettle
- ❏ Drill
- ❏ 1/2" drill bit
- ❏ Lightweight potting mix
- ❏ Plants
- ❏ Mulch

HOW TO MAKE IT

1. Drill some holes in the bottom and sides of your tea kettle.
2. Fill the kettle half full with potting mix.
3. Loosen plant roots and place plants in the potting mix.
4. Top up with potting mix and a layer of mulch.
5. Water well.

TIP: Collect a number of different styles of antique tea kettles and make a dramatic display.

Rose-Stuffed Purse

Admit it, you have more than one unused purse sitting in the dark recesses of your closet that you just can't bear to throw away. In fact, you most likely already have the perfect bag just lying in wait for this pretty and creative project! If not, funky and unique purses are a dime a dozen at your local thrift shop.

WHAT YOU NEED

- ❑ Old purse
- ❑ Scissors
- ❑ Small pebbles
- ❑ Lightweight potting mix
- ❑ Plants
- ❑ Mulch

HOW TO MAKE IT

1. Cut a few slits for drainage in the bottom of the purse.

2. Pour about a half inch of small pebbles in the bottom of the purse, enough to line the bottom.

3. Fill the purse about halfway with potting mix.

4. Loosen plant roots and place plants in the potting mix.

5. Top with a light layer of potting mix and mulch.

6. Water well.

TIP: Fill several purses and line them along a fence or your back patio for an eye-catching display.

Not Your Ordinary Drawer

Whoever said that dressers could only be for clothes? Grab some paint and ornate handles and class up a dresser drawer for an interesting container garden. Use chalk paint and distress the edges with sandpaper to breathe new life into an old drawer. Try stacking various sizes of drawers to create an interesting staggered look.

WHAT YOU NEED

- ❑ Drawer
- ❑ Drill
- ❑ 1/2" drill bit
- ❑ Lightweight potting mix
- ❑ Plants
- ❑ River rock

HOW TO MAKE IT

1. Drill at least six drainage holes in the bottom and along the sides of the drawer.

2. Line the bottom of the drawer with a light layer of river rock. This will help with drainage.

3. Fill the drawer about halfway with potting mix.

4. Loosen plant roots and place plants in the potting mix.

5. Top with a light layer of river rock.

6. Water well.

TIP: Don't stop with just one drawer! Fill a whole chest of drawers with plants for a real focal point on your patio or deck.

Little Red Wagon

This little red wagon can be wheeled around to any spot in your yard. Fill it up with shade plants, sun plants, or a mix of both and keep them all happy by moving the wagon as required. Not to mention that this gem takes you back to your childhood and adds a classic vintage touch to your garden paradise.

WHAT YOU NEED

- ❑ Wagon (the older the better!)
- ❑ Drill
- ❑ 1" drill bit
- ❑ Lightweight potting mix
- ❑ Plants
- ❑ Mulch

HOW TO MAKE IT

1. Drill drainage holes in the bottom and sides of the wagon.
2. Fill wagon halfway with potting mix.
3. Loosen roots of plants and add to the potting mix.
4. Top with more potting mix and mulch.
5. Water well.

TIP: If you can find three wagons—one large, one medium, and one small-sized—group them together for a focal point on your patio or deck.

Bundtastic

Let's be honest, we all have at least one bundt pan gifted by a well-meaning relative...and it's collecting dust and spider webs in the back of our kitchen cabinets. Rather than waiting until the appropriate time has passed and reluctantly digging it out for your next yard sale, turn those unused kitchen pans into beautiful planters that are sure to add shine and sophistication to any garden.

WHAT YOU NEED

- ❑ Bundt pan
- ❑ Drill
- ❑ 1/8" drill bit
- ❑ Lightweight potting mix
- ❑ Plants
- ❑ Mulch

HOW TO MAKE IT

1. Drill some drainage holes in your bundt pan.
2. Fill the pan halfway with potting mix.
3. Loosen the roots on plants and add to the potting mix.
4. Top with more potting mix and mulch.
5. Water well.

TIP: Get really creative and take advantage of the big hole in the middle of the bundt pan by putting a tall pillar candle in it.

Flower Shower

Where watering cans were once used to bring life-giving water to your flowers, now they can provide life in a different way. Turn a dysfunctional or antique watering can into a new home for your colorful flowers. Plus, as an added bonus, watering cans come in many different colors and shapes and can add immense variety to your garden.

WHAT YOU NEED

- ❑ Old watering can (plastic or metal)
- ❑ Drill
- ❑ 1/8" drill bit
- ❑ Lightweight potting mix
- ❑ Plants
- ❑ Mulch

HOW TO MAKE IT

1. Drill drainage holes in the bottom and along the sides of the watering can.
2. Fill the can halfway with potting mix.
3. Loosen the roots of the plants and add to the potting mix.
4. Top with more potting mix and mulch.
5. Water well.

TIP: Get really funky with this project and attach your can at an angle to a post for a dramatic focal point in your garden.

Just Hangin' Around

For this project, I used a unique piece of old wood I had hanging around and a couple of little metal containers from a yard sale. The finished piece has a cool rustic feel to it. This project really allows you to express your creativity; any buckets, containers, or bins that can be attached to wood could make an awesome planter. You could even try painting the wood with a design or a different color.

- Piece of cool wood
- Sandpaper (or sanding block)
- Clean rag
- Stain (optional)
- Metal container to mount on wood
- Drill
- Drill bit (unless your containers have drainage holes already)
- Small nails (pick what works for your wood depth)
- Screws
- Screwdriver
- Hammer
- Chain
- Lightweight potting soil
- Plants
- Mulch

HOW TO MAKE IT

1. Sand any rough spots off of the wood and wipe the wood down.
2. Attach the chin to the back of the wood using appropriate size screws.
3. Stain the wood if desired and allow it to dry.
4. Drill drainage holes in your containers, unless they already have holes.
5. Nail your containers to the wood (check for best nail depth).
6. Fill containers halfway with lightweight potting mix.
7. Loosen plant roots and place in the soil.
8. Cover with more soil and a light layer of mulch.
9. Water well.

TIP: This project works best when you use containers that have flat backs so that they sit flush against the wood.

Stumped

No one likes unsightly stumps cluttering up their yard or garden. Unfortunately, however, there is often not much that can be done to remove these tree remnants. Particularly when they're from ancient, deeply-rooted trees. So rather than trying to conceal your stumps, embrace them and turn them into something beautiful once again. This project takes some time, so be patient!

WHAT YOU NEED

- ☐ Drill
- ☐ 16" drill bit
- ☐ Wood-boring tri flute spade drill bit
- ☐ Paddle bit
- ☐ Vacuum
- ☐ Dry stump
- ☐ Lightweight potting mix
- ☐ Plants
- ☐ Mulch

HOW TO MAKE IT

1. Bore holes in the top end of the stump. Use the widest paddle bit to get the biggest and deepest holes. Keep drilling to at least eight inches and desired width.

2. Vacuum out the shavings from time to time as you drill.

3. Create a drainage hole in the log using the paddle bit.

4. Fill the planting hole halfway with lightweight potting mix.

5. Loosen the roots of the plants and place in soil.

6. Top with potting soil and mulch.

7. Water well.

TIP: If you happen to have three stumps or logs of various sizes, fill them all with flowers for an eye-catching display.

Take A Seat

There's just something about old chairs being used for things other than their intended purpose that seems so appealing and unique. Forget sitting around the dinner table! Turn your old, seatless chairs into a work of art that will become a conversation piece. Use these in the back of your garden where more height can add a lovely focal point.

WHAT YOU NEED

- ❑ Old chair with or without the inner seat
- ❑ Pot that will fit inside the chair hole
- ❑ Lightweight potting mix
- ❑ Plants

HOW TO MAKE IT

1. If you have a chair with an inner seat, remove the seat so that there is a hole for the pot.
2. Plant your flowers in your pot. Be sure that there is plenty of drainage. If your pot does not have drainage holes, make some.
3. Place your chair in the best location for the plants you have chosen.
4. Set your container inside the seat of the chair.
5. Water well.

TIP: Place moss around the seat before you put the pot in the hole.

"Where flowers bloom, so does hope."
— Lady Bird Johnson

TIPS FOR GROWING VEGGIES IN CONTAINERS

"It's difficult to think anything but pleasant thoughts while eating a homegrown tomato." — **Lewis Grizzard**

There is nothing quite like the taste of homegrown vegetables picked right from your own garden. Not everyone has the space or desire for a big garden, but that doesn't mean you have to miss out! Container veggie and fruit gardening offer an opportunity for anyone to enjoy the gardening experience in a small space.

On the next few pages you will find tips for growing both vegetables in containers. Follow these tips for a bountiful harvest right on your very own patio or back deck.

Lots Of Sun

The majority of veggie plants like a least six hours of sun. When you are deciding where to locate your containers, keep this in mind.

Cool Roots

While sun is important, you have to be careful that plant roots don't get too hot. In a container, roots receive radiant heat from the sun, unlike plants in a conventional garden. If you live in a very hot climate, it is wise to consider some afternoon shade for the plants. This can be accomplished by moving them to a shady area or erecting a shade cloth.

Containers Matter

Never plant vegetables in metal containers—they radiate too much heat! Neutral-colored pots are best. Be sure that pots have plenty of drainage. Cover drainage holes inside the pot with a piece of mesh fabric to keep insects out. Be sure to select pots that reflect the mature size of the veggie plant. Plants that do not have enough space to mature will become rootbound and unhealthy.

Don't Crowd

As mentioned above, veggies need space to grow. Pay attention to the space distance recommended for your plants and follow this when planting. Putting too many plants in one pot will result in crowding and competition for water and nutrients. This will result in stunted growth and small fruit.

Soil Mix

When preparing your containers for planting, it is critical to consider high-quality soil that contains a lot of organic matter. Don't ever take soil from your garden as it could contain seeds and remnants of bacteria that might impact your container plant. Choose a high-quality lightweight soil mixture. I use a combination of equal parts perlite, potting soil, and compost in all my containers.

Water

Veggies require quite a bit of water, but not too much. Root rot and disease will set in if you overwater. To know when to water, stick your finger down into the soil to your knuckle. If it feels dry, it's time to water.

Never water plants when they are in full sun. Two things happen when you water during the heat of the day. First, your plants will boil with the radiant heat. Second, your watering will be quite ineffective as most of it will evaporate. The best time to water is in the early morning hours or just after sunset.

Mulch

I always add a one-inch layer of lightweight mulch to all veggie containers. This mulch serves as a protective layer. It keeps the soil and roots cool, retains moisture, and also adds a nice decorative touch.

Growing Zone

Familiarize yourself with what grows best in your region, when to plant, and what challenges you may face. There is nothing more frustrating than planting something out of season or out of your growing zone.

TIPS FOR GROWING FRUIT IN CONTAINERS

" Share fruit with friends and your heart will be warmed."

Many people shy away from growing fruit in containers because they think that they need lots of room. However, there are many fruit types, including dwarf varieties, that do very well in containers set on a patio or even in a sunny and warm room in the house. Here are a few tips to ensure your success growing fruit in containers.

Use Dwarf Plants

When shopping for a fruit tree or bush, look for a dwarf or semi-dwarf type. Dwarf trees will only grow to be about eight feet tall and compact fruit bush varieties are well-suited to containers. The great thing is that dwarf-type fruit trees and bushes produce just as much fruit as their regular-sized counterparts.

Remember Drainage

Like any plant in a pot, fruit trees and bushes require a pot with plenty of drainage. Keep in mind that if your pot is going to sit on a solid surface, you will want to put drainage holes near the bottom of the pot on both sides.

High-Quality Soil

A mixture of high-quality potting soil and compost will give your fruit trees and bushes plenty of nutrients to start growing well in a container.

Top It Up

Fruit trees and bushes do well with a top layer of mulch to help keep roots cool and soil moist. It is best to use lightweight mulch or even peat moss.

Consider Winter

If you are growing a dwarf fruit tree or fruit bush that will not survive the winter in the area you live in, be sure to have a plan. If you are growing berries, you can sink the pots in your compost pile up to the rim to keep them warm. Or place a wire fence around the container and fill the inside with mulch to protect the plant. Berries will also overwinter in an unheated garage. Just be sure to water your berry plant once in February.

Sack of Potatoes

As any avid vegetable gardener knows, potatoes grow especially well in bags. However, there's no need to purchase a special potato bag when you can make your own from recycled coffee sacks. Not only are coffee sacks cute and come in various sizes, they are also extremely sturdy and will last for at least a couple of growing seasons.

HOW TO MAKE IT

1. Roll the edges of your sack down to make a short bag about six inches high.

2. Fill with five inches of loose potting mix.

3. Place your potatoes on top of the potting mix about six inches apart, eyes facing upwards.

4. Cover potatoes with six inches of soil.

TIP: In a couple of weeks, you will see the leafy plant push up through the soil. At this time, mound the soil around the plant to promote more growth. Leave a little bit of green about the soil. For best results, keep the soil moist but not soaking. If you live in a rainy climate, you will want to shelter your bag to prevent too much moisture. Harvest in eighty to 100 days by dumping your sack over.

Hanging Plastic Pipe Planter

In some yards, space is not a luxury to be hogged by massive container gardens. In those instances, or if you just want to add color, creative flair, and personality to your area, take advantage of this plan for hanging planters. You can choose to use these for fruits and vegetables like lettuce, strawberries, and greens, or plant gorgeous flowers for aesthetic purposes.

Note: If vegetables, fruits, or herbs are grown in this container, it is important that you use a food grade HDPE #5 pipe.

WHAT YOU NEED

- 3 pieces of 4" pipe, 3 feet long
- Six 4" end caps
- 10 eyelets (screw-in type)
- 8-feet chain of your choosing (to hang planter)
- Drill
- 2" drill bit
- 1/8" drill bit for drain holes
- 1/16" drill bit for eyelets
- 2 pairs of pliers (to separate chain)
- Marker
- Tape measure
- Spray paint
- Lightweight potting mix
- Plants

HOW TO MAKE IT

1. On each pipe, use a tape measure to pinpoint three inches from both ends and make a mark. On two of the pipes, make a mark on the top and the bottom.

2. Using the 1/16" drill bit, drill holes for eyelets at your marks from step one.

3. Using the 1/8" drill bit, drill twelve holes spaced evenly on the underside of each piece of pipe (for drainage).

4. Paint pipes with the color of your choice.

5. Install the eyelets in the holes you made in step two.

6. Attach chain to each eyelet.

7. Using the 2" drill bit, drill holes on the topside of pipe to hold plants.

8. Hang planter horizontally.

9. Fill each hole with lightweight soil.

10. Place your plants in each pipe.

11. Water well.

TIP: Run an irrigation hose through the pipes for irrigation.

Potato Crate

Pretty much anyone who has ever built anything has random scraps of wood lying around on their property. So gather your wood and a few nails and throw these crates together, or scrounge up some old wooden crates from another source. These compact, convenient potato planters prevent your tubers from disappearing into the ground and keeps them fresh throughout the growing season.

WHAT YOU NEED

- ☐ Old wooden crate (4'x4' is the best size)
- ☐ Nail bar (or cat's claw)
- ☐ Shredded newspaper
- ☐ Lightweight potting soil
- ☐ Seed potatoes

HOW TO MAKE IT

1. Remove the bottom from the old crate using a nail bar or a cat's claw. Safely dispose of the nails.

2. Set the crate in a location where it will receive at least six hours of sunlight per day.

3. Place a two-inch layer of shredded newspaper in the bottom of the box.

4. Set seed potatoes cut-side down and six inches apart on the newspaper.

5. Cover potatoes with two inches of potting mix.

6. When the plants grow six inches above the soil, place another three-inch layer of potting mix on top. Repeat this process until you have reached the top of the box.

7. Water the potatoes so that the soil is consistently wet, but not soggy. It is best to water each time you add a new layer.

8. Feed potatoes throughout the growing season with a balanced organic fertilizer.

TIP: When potatoes are ready to be harvested, simply lift the box up! No digging required.

Gutter Garden

Keeping runner plants like strawberries contained can be difficult. They tend to creep under even the most resilient of barriers and can spread to every corner of your garden. However, an old gutter can eliminate any overpowering problems and provide a convenient place for strawberry harvesting. Attach the strip of gutter to your fence or leave it resting on the ground for added color.

WHAT YOU NEED

- Piece of guttering (you can ask around or check your local Craigslist for pieces of non-rusted guttering material)
- Scrub brush
- Paint
- Drill
- 1" drill bit
- Screws for attaching (be sure you use the right material depending on where you are placing your gutter garden)
- Lightweight potting mix
- Strawberries
- Mulch

HOW TO MAKE IT

1. Clean the gutter and be sure there is no flaking paint or other debris.

2. Drill drainage holes every inch along the bottom of the gutter.

3. Paint your gutter to match your decor (spray paint works best).

4. Attach the guttering to the chosen location. Add screws to keep the guttering firmly in place.

5. Fill the gutter three-quarters full with lightweight potting mix.

6. Plant strawberries and add more potting mix.

7. Top with mulch.

8. Water well.

TIP: Add some pretty annuals in with your strawberries for a dazzling display.

Pipe Vertical Growing Tower

If you are short on space, this vertical strawberry or succulent planter is a perfect choice. You can put this on your patio or deck and expect a boatload of strawberries come harvest time. Paint each tower a different color or create a uniform set of pipe planters at different heights. Put this in the back of your garden for some added height.

Note: If vegetables, fruits, or herbs are grown in this container, it is important that you use a food grade HDPE #5 pipe.

WHAT YOU NEED

- [ ] 4" pipe, 6 feet long
- [ ] Shovel
- [ ] Drill
- [ ] 2" drill bit
- [ ] Spray paint
- [ ] Level
- [ ] Lightweight potting mix
- [ ] Plants

HOW TO MAKE IT

1. Spray paint the pipe and let it dry.
2. Dig a sixteen-inch hole to accommodate the pipe.
3. Put the pipe in the ground and fill in the hole. Use a level to be sure the pipe is level.
4. Using the 2" drill bit, place holes in various locations on the pipe.
5. Fill the pipe with moist, lightweight potting mix.
6. Place your plants in the pipe.
7. Water well.

A mix of succulents and strawberries are growing in this vertical planter.

TIP: Run a soaker hose through this pipe for irrigation.

Bucket of Berries

Pretty much everyone has access to a five-gallon bucket. If you don't have one floating around your yard, they are pretty inexpensive to purchase. These buckets are easy to dress up with burlap or paint to suit your garden decor.

- ❑ 5-gallon container (or larger)
- ❑ Drill and 1/2" drill bit
- ❑ Lightweight potting mix
- ❑ High acid potting mix
- ❑ Dwarf, self-pollinating blueberry bush
- ❑ Mulch

HOW TO MAKE IT

1. Drill drainage holes near the bottom of the bucket, all the way around.

2. Fill the container two-thirds full with lightweight potting mix.

3. Loosen roots on the blueberry bush and place them in the pot.

4. Cover the bush with a high acid potting mix.

5. Top with a light layer of mulch.

6. Water well.

7. Set your pot in a sunny spot. Blueberries like at least six hours of sun per day.

TIP: To protect your pots from hungry birds, place a lightweight netting around your plant when it is about to set fruit.

Peek-A-Bamboo

Something about bamboo just screams tiki torches and beachside vacations. But have you ever tried bringing the tropics to your own yard? This inventive bamboo planter is the perfect place to grow lettuce, succulents, and other shallow-rooted plants. Attach it to the fence with hangers so that you can move it or bring it inside as the weather changes.

- ❏ 4" bamboo, 3 feet piece
- ❏ Drill
- ❏ 1/2"drill bit
- ❏ 1/8" drill bit
  (for drainage holes)
- ❏ Jigsaw
- ❏ Sandpaper
- ❏ Marker
- ❏ Screws
  (to attach to wall or fence)
- ❏ Lightweight potting mix
- ❏ Plants

HOW TO MAKE IT

1. Mark on the top side of the bamboo where you wish to place your plants.

2. Using 1/2" drill bit, start a pilot hole at each spot.

3. Using the jigsaw, cut out the desired opening.

4. Sand edges of the holes.

5. Using 1/8" drill bit, make holes on the underside of the bamboo for drainage.

6. Attach the planter to the wall or fence using appropriate screws.

TIP: Use food-grade oil to moisturize inside of bamboo before planting.

Wrapped Pepper Pot

With this container garden, your pepper plants will have a place to grow along the trellis. It is very convenient to have vegetable plants located at strategic places along your patio rather than squished together in some corner vegetable garden. This allows for ease of harvest, watering, and pest control. Plus, printed burlap sacks are timeless and add a vintage feel to any garden.

WHAT YOU NEED

- ❑ Burlap sack
- ❑ Scissors
- ❑ Pepper plant in a pot
  with trellis

HOW TO MAKE IT

1. Cut the sack open.

2. Wrap the sack around
   the pot.

3. Water the pepper plant well.
   Fertilize every three weeks
   with an organic fertilizer
   during the growing season.

TIP: Keep in mind that pepper plants grown in pots mature quicker than those planted in the garden. Harvesting early will encourage more fruit to set.

Bottled

Though we can try our hardest, sometimes plastic waste is inevitable. But rather than let your bottles languish in landfills, recycle them into costless, eco-friendly planters. Each season, use a bunch of these scattered throughout your growing area or clustered together for an easy harvest. Please note, this type of planter is best for shallow-rooted veggies like lettuce and other greens.

"The glory of gardening: hands in the dirt, head in the sun, heart with nature. To nurture a garden is to feed not just the body, but the soul."
— Alfred Austin

- ❑ 33.8-ounce plastic bottle
- ❑ Sharp scissors
- ❑ Drill
- ❑ 1/8" drill bit
- ❑ Heavy duty string (or wire)
- ❑ Lightweight potting soil
- ❑ Plants

HOW TO MAKE IT

1. Wash plastic bottle well and allow it to dry.
2. Cut a three-inch by two-inch hole in the center.
3. Drill one hole in the top and bottom of the bottle near the ends (for stringing).
4. Drill a few holes in the bottom of the bottle for drainage.
5. Fill bottle partway with lightweight potting mix.
6. Add plants and cover with lightweight potting soil.
7. Water well.

TIP: Gather multiple bottles and string them together for an abundant vertical garden.

Hanging Tomato In Wicker

Tomatoes are right at home in any type of hanging basket. There are a few varieties that love to hang around, but Romas and Tumbling Toms are my favorite. It is so much fun walking by this basket and plucking off a delicious, homegrown tomato. Hang tomatoes in a sunny location on your patio and watch them take off!

- ❑ Hanging basket with a moss or coconut husk liner
- ❑ Hook for hanging
- ❑ Lightweight potting soil
- ❑ Tomato plant
- ❑ Mulch

HOW TO MAKE IT

1. Decide on a good location for your hanging tomato plant. Preferably somewhere that receives at least four to six hours of sunlight per day.

2. Install a hook for hanging the basket.

3. Fill the container about halfway with lightweight potting mix.

4. Loosen roots on tomato plant and place in basket.

5. Cover with lightweight potting mix and mulch.

6. Water well.

TIP: For best results, place the tomato plant in a hole that is slightly deeper than its root ball.

Basketful of Lettuce

Baskets aren't just good for carrying food on picnics, they are often amazing for growing the food you will take on the picnics as well. Whether you have unused baskets lying around, or find some at a second-hand store, woven baskets are not very hard to find. Plus, with the handles, this container garden is extremely portable and can easily be carried to whatever destination you desire.

WHAT YOU NEED

- ☐ Basket at least 8" deep
- ☐ Lightweight plastic sheeting (if your basket does not have a liner)
- ☐ Scissors
- ☐ Lightweight potting mix
- ☐ Mulch
- ☐ Lettuce

HOW TO MAKE IT

1. If your basket does not have a liner, cut a piece of plastic sheeting to fit inside the basket.

2. Cut a few small holes in the bottom of the liner to allow for drainage.

3. Fill the basket halfway with lightweight potting mix.

4. Loosen the lettuce roots and place in potting mix.

5. Cover with more potting mix and a light layer of mulch.

6. Water well.

TIP: Lettuce loves sunlight, but if you live in a particularly hot region, give your container some afternoon shade.

Pallet Perfection

Finding pallets for projects is easy. Ripping them up and upcycling them, however, is not often worth the effort. Thankfully, this pallet garden requires no deconstruction or building skills and can be assembled in just a few minutes. Fill this bed with colorful hanging vines or delicious herbs and veggies to maximize its full potential.

WHAT YOU NEED

- ☐ Nail bar
- ☐ Wooden pallet in good shape
- ☐ Scissors
- ☐ Garden fabric
- ☐ Organic potting soil
- ☐ Staple gun and staples
- ☐ Plants

HOW TO MAKE IT

1. Check the pallet for any nails that are sticking out and remove them.

2. Turn the pallet over.

3. Lay garden fabric on the back.

4. Allow enough excess to cover all four sides at the end and the top.

5. Trim the fabric.

6. Staple the fabric to the back of the pallet. It is great to have a helper for this part to hold the fabric taut. Staple the outer edges first. Put additional staples on the center beams.

7. Turn the pallet over and staple the top. The idea is to seal all places where dirt could escape, apart from the front side.

8. Position your pallet bed in the desired location.

9. Fill the pallet bed with soil and plants.

10. Water well.

GROWING HERBS IN CONTAINERS

"Fresh herbs really do belong anywhere you put them." — Alex Guarnaschelli

The beautiful thing about growing herbs in containers is that there is no green thumb required. In fact, growing herbs in containers is an amazing confidence booster for anyone. Whether you have a few containers on your balcony or in a sunny inside window, herbs will reward you with their lush growth and aromatic pleasures.

Here are a few other things I have learned growing herbs over the years that will help your experience be fun and rewarding.

Get Picky

Pick herbs often during the growing season. Although you may be tempted to let herbs get big and tall, picking them will result in a fuller and healthier plant. Don't pick stems from the base of the plant, this will cause the plant to grow tall and lanky. To pick herbs correctly, pick off the tips of each stem one or two inches above a pair of leaves. This will promote new shoots from each stem and a healthy and bushy plant.

Feed Well

The second rule for successful herb container gardening is to feed herbs using a half-strength liquid seaweed or worm tea every three weeks during their growing season. Liquid seaweed is loaded with minerals and trace elements that boost healthy herb growth and promote great flavor.

Choose Well

Plant selection matters. Picking the healthiest herbs from the start will help ensure that your adult plant is also healthy and productive. Purchase your herbs from a reputable grower or grow yours from high-quality seeds.

Possible Pots

While herbs will grow in just about any container, assuming that it has adequate drainage, some herbs do better in certain types of pots than others. If you wish to plant perennial herbs outside in a permanent display, don't choose plastic—it will deteriorate over time. If you plant moisture-loving herbs, avoid clay pots that tend to draw moisture and dry herbs out quickly. Clay pots will also break during a hard frost.

You can grow a single herb in a pot as small as ten inches in diameter. For bigger herbs or multiple plants, use a pot at least eighteen inches in diameter. Keep in mind that providing a bigger container for your herb will result in a bigger plant.

Best Planting Medium

Regular garden soil is too heavy for container herbs. Instead, choose a lightweight potting medium that will retain moisture and drain well. Here is my favorite mixture that I use for my herbs:

- One part commercial potting mix
- One part aged manure
- One part coarse sand

This mixture is light, nutrient-rich, and drains great!

Perfect Pairing

Growing multiple herbs in the same pot can make a really attractive display. Be sure to pair herbs that have similar light and water requirements together. Also, pair plants based on their mature size and be sure to give them plenty of room for expansion.

Creative Container Placement

I love to get creative with my herb container placement. A container or two at the front door welcomes guests with a burst of aromatic pleasure. I also like to group containers of various sizes for a focal point on my deck, place containers in gaps in my gardens, or place them along paths in my landscape. Besides growing containers in your kitchen window, think outside the box. Use herbs to bring beauty to other bright areas in and around your home.

Drain and Strain

Let's be honest, no one really knows the culinary purpose of those tiny colanders that can barely hold a noodle. This Greek oregano, however, is very much at home in this petite colander. Set this little container garden on your back patio or in your kitchen window for an attractive accent piece and easy access while cooking.

- ☐ Colander
- ☐ Lightweight potting soil
- ☐ Herbs
- ☐ Mulch

HOW TO MAKE IT

1. Fill the colander halfway with lightweight potting soil.

2. Loosen plant roots and place in the soil.

3. Top with soil and mulch.

4. Water well.

TIP: Display this colander of herbs inside. Place a decorative or vintage plate underneath to catch drainage.

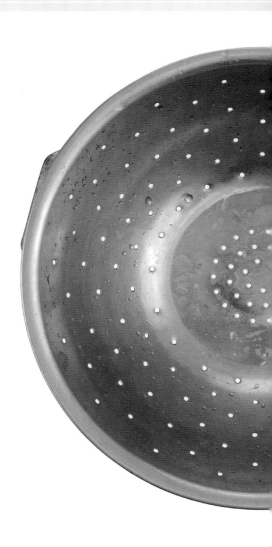

Basketful of Goodness

This beautiful basket is loaded with herbs. It can rest nicely on any sunny kitchen counter or on your kitchen table for easy access when cooking. Any basket will do as long as your herb pots will fit inside. Try mixing a few different types of herbs to experience all the flavors of a natural pantry.

- ☐ Basket
- ☐ Herbs in pots

HOW TO MAKE IT

1. Choose a basket to your liking.
2. Place herb pots in basket.
3. Water well.

TIP: Take herb containers out of the basket and water deeply two to three times a week as needed. Keep plants healthy and full by pinching leaves off regularly.

Always cooks up
WHITE and FLUFFY

Nostalgic Tin

Packaging just used to be so much more interesting. Ah, well, rather than lament the cardboard and plastic containers of today, let's take a moment and pay homage to the cookie, rice, and popcorn tins of the past. Keep an eagle eye out for cute containers such as these at yard sales and thrift stores.

WHAT YOU NEED

- ❑ Tin of any kind (preferably something cool and light in color)
- ❑ Drill
- ❑ 1/2" drill bit
- ❑ Pebbles
- ❑ Lightweight potting mix
- ❑ Herbs

HOW TO MAKE IT

1. If your chosen tin does not have drainage, make some holes on the sides of the container near the bottom.
2. Add a layer of pebbles to the bottom of the tin.
3. Fill the tin about halfway with lightweight potting mix.
4. Loosen roots of plants and place in tin.
5. Water well.

TIP: To keep your herbs healthy, pinch them back or use regularly.

ROIT

Crate It Up

Wooden crates are probably the most versatile container garden. They can be designed to fit any yard style and classed up to look more modern if necessary. After a while, you will notice crates becoming a staple in your gardening techniques, adding texture, interest, and that ever-elusive eclectic vibe.

WHAT YOU NEED

- Sturdy wooden crate
- Linseed oil
- Rag
- Drill
- 1/2" drill bit (maybe)
- Porous landscape fabric
- Scissors
- Lightweight potting soil
- Herbs (appropriate for the depth and size of your crate)
- River rocks or pebbles

HOW TO MAKE IT

1. Apply the linseed oil to the outside and inside of the wooden crate. This will help preserve the wood.

2. After your crate has dried, fill it with water and check how long it takes for the water to run out. If it runs out freely, you don't need drainage holes. If not, add drainage holes on the bottom and sides of the crate.

3. Cut a piece of landscape fabric to fit in the bottom and up the sides of the wooden crate.

4. Fill the crate halfway with lightweight potting soil.

5. Loosen plant roots and place them in the soil.

6. Cover with soil and a light layer of pebbles or river rocks.

7. Water well.

TIP: Look for old wooden milk crates– they already have dividers built in!

Barnwood Bamboo Mount

Rustic barnwood is becoming all the rage. If you are looking for an easy container garden to turn your backyard into a shabby chic masterpiece, this project is for you. Bamboo succulent mounts can be arranged along a fence or staggered at different heights to bring life to a boring wood boundary marker.

WHAT YOU NEED

- ❑ Piece of rustic wood or barn wood of your choosing
- ❑ 4" bamboo end pieces, cut to your desired length (x2)
- ❑ Wood screws
- ❑ Drill
- ❑ 1/8" drill bit
- ❑ Lightweight potting mix
- ❑ Herbs

HOW TO MAKE IT

1. Using 1/8" drill bit, drill drainage holes in bottom or side of bamboo pieces.

2. Attach bamboo to the rustic wood from the backside. (Be careful of the exposed screw end when you plant.)

3. Attach wood to the desired location.

4. Fill bamboo with lightweight potting soil.

5. Loosen plant roots and place plants in containers.

6. Water well.

TIP: Make sure that the bamboo is a closed cell.

Bamboo Living Picture

Container gardening is often about how to most seamlessly bring the indoors outdoors. How to make your patio and garden area an extension of your indoor living space. This garden certainly accomplishes that by combining a faux picture frame with the end of a stalk of bamboo. You may even decide you like this project so much that you want to keep it hanging on your wall inside as a conversation starter.

WHAT YOU NEED

- Old picture frame without back and glass
- Wood glue (to glue in wood for the back side)
- Old pieces of thin wood (to fill in the back of the frame)
- 4" bamboo piece with end cell (desired size)
- Drill
- 1/8" drill bit
- Screws
- Vegetable oil
- Rag
- Lightweight potting mix
- Plants

HOW TO MAKE IT

1. Assemble your picture frame using thin wood and glue. (You can also use small hand nails.)

2. Using 1/8" drill bit, make drainage holes in sides, near bottom of bamboo.

3. Using screws, attach bamboo to picture frame from the backside.

4. Using a rag, apply a thin layer of vegetable oil to the inside of the bamboo container.

5. Hang your picture container using appropriate fasteners.

6. Fill bamboo with lightweight potting mix.

7. Loosen plant roots and place in the potting mix.

8. Water well.

TIP: For fun, try wood burning a design on your bamboo container.

Mason Jar Mint

This project is really designed to get those creative juices flowing. Experiment with different ways to paint your mason jars or decorate them with various items, such as shells, layered in the soil. You could even try giving these out as gifts for events or just because. Try using different plants to add variety and keep fresh herbs available for all your cooking needs.

- ❏ Mason jars
- ❏ Glass paint
- ❏ Drill and 1/8" glass-cutting drill bit
- ❏ Masking tape
- ❏ Pebbles
- ❏ Lightweight potting mix
- ❏ Herbs

HOW TO MAKE IT

1. Spray paint the mason jars and let them dry.

2. Place a piece of masking tape around the jar near the bottom.

3. Drill six drainage holes.

4. Put pebbles in the bottom of the jar.

5. Fill the jar partway with lightweight potting soil.

6. Loosen the roots on plants and place in jar.

7. Top with lightweight potting mix and more pebbles if desired.

8. Water well.

TIP: Instead of gravel, line the bottom of the jar with marbles for drainage. This is especially decorative if you choose not to paint your jar.

Wash 'N Grow

It doesn't get much simpler than this: a used dish wash basin becomes home to herbs and annual flowers. This low-cost project makes a great addition to any deck or patio and allows even those with the smallest balcony to enjoy fresh herbs and beautiful blooms all season long. Plus, you can try adding colorful pebbles to make the display more appealing.

- ❑ Old wash pan
- ❑ Drill
- ❑ 1/2" drill bit
- ❑ Pebbles
- ❑ Lightweight potting mix
- ❑ Herbs

HOW TO MAKE IT

1. Drill drainage holes in each side of the wash pan near the bottom.

2. Line the bottom of the wash pan with pebbles.

3. Top the pebbles with lightweight potting soil. Fill the container about halfway.

4. Loosen roots on plants and place them in the potting mix.

5. Cover with more potting mix and pebbles.

6. Water well.

TIP: Select a lighter-colored washtub to keep the plant roots cool.

Notes 'N Such

This adorable container not only serves as a home for your bountiful herbs, it also could be the source of much encouragement and laughter. Get creative with the notes you leave on the board and make a game out of it with yourself or with your family members. This living message board is sure to become a beloved staple in the home as you watch and nurture the plants within.

WHAT YOU NEED

- 1x8x16" piece of wood (x4)
- 1x8x8" piece of wood (x2)
- 1x1/2x12" piece of wood (x2)
- Finish nails
- Hammer
- Screws
- Drill
- 1/4" drill bit (for drainage holes)
- Chalkboard paint
- 8x16" picture frame
- 8x16" piece of 1/4" plywood (smooth)
- Paint for box
- Decor for box
- Lightweight potting soil
- Plants

HOW TO MAKE IT

1. Form a box using two 1x8x16" pieces of wood and 1x8x8" pieces of wood. Nail it together.

2. Using the remaining 1x8x16" pieces of wood, attach them to the bottom of the box.

3. Using a 1/8" drill bit, make drainage holes on the sides of the box.

4. Paint the wood using chalkboard paint and allow it to dry.

5. Attach the wood to the picture frame using finish nails.

6. Attach the 1x1/2" piece of wood to either side of the picture frame.

7. Paint and decorate the box, then allow it to dry.

8. Attach the picture frame to the box using appropriate screws.

9. Add lightweight potting mix and herbs.

10. Water well.

TIP: If you're using the frame inside, line the inside of the box with plastic sheeting.

Wheelbarrow Full of Herbs

Perhaps one of the most common container gardens, there has long been a trend of planting a flower bed in your wash-up wheelbarrow. Just because it can no longer assist you in your garden work, doesn't mean it has any less of a role to play in your backyard haven. Turn an old, falling apart wheelbarrow into a beautiful place for herbs, or a new annual bed each year.

WHAT YOU NEED

- ☐ Old wheelbarrow
- ☐ Drill
- ☐ 1" drill bit
- ☐ Lightweight potting mix
- ☐ Plants
- ☐ Mulch

HOW TO MAKE IT

1. Drill at least one hole every two inches in the bottom of the wheelbarrow for drainage (unless you already have plenty of drainage).

2. If you can't move the wheelbarrow, be sure to position it where you want it in your landscape.

3. Line the bottom of the wheelbarrow with a one-inch layer of gravel or pebbles.

4. Fill the wheelbarrow with lightweight potting mix.

5. Lay out your plants, thinking about which plants do well together and make a nice display.

6. Loosen the roots on plants and place them in the potting mix.

7. Cover plants with more potting mix and top with a layer of mulch.

8. Water well.

TIP: Plant the tallest plants in the middle of the wheelbarrow if the display is going to be seen from all sides. Mix some pretty annual flowers in with the herbs for color.

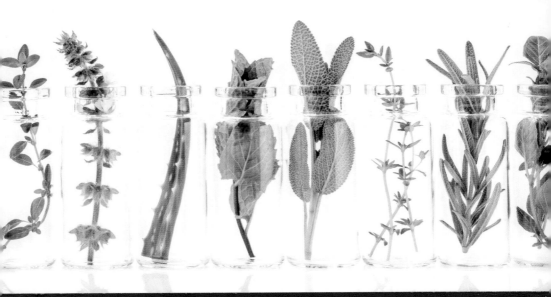

GROWING SUCCULENTS IN CONTAINERS

"Ask, and the succulent will tell you how to stay beautiful despite adversity."
— Susan Patterson (author)

I decided to include this bonus section on creating succulent container gardens because they are so near and dear to my heart. I took an avid interest in succulents when I moved out to the west and began to use them in my garden as well as inside my home.

There is a wide variety of succulents to choose from, each differing in size, texture, and color. One of the most beautiful things about succulents is that they are easy to care for and often thrive with little or no attention.

Succulents get their name from their ability to store water for a long period of time in their leaves, roots, and stems. This broad category of plants includes the well-known aloe plant, cacti, snake plant, mini rosettes, and so many more.

Depending on where you live, some succulents can survive outdoors, while others prefer warmer temperatures and will need to come indoors with inclement weather. Know the needs of your succulents before planting them.

Here are a few tips to keep in mind for fabulous succulent container gardens:

- Plant above the rim. Succulents will be the healthiest when they sit just above the rim of your container.
- Space or no space. You can plant succulents close together or give them space, whichever suits your container.
- Use trailing succulents. Make your container gardens more interesting by using some trailing succulents that will hang over the edge of the container.
- Don't be too attentive. Succulent gardens are independent, meaning they don't like to be fussed over.
- Cover drainage holes with landscape fabric. This will improve drainage and soil retention.
- Water them during growing season. Water succulents in the spring and summer. It is best to let the soil dry out before watering.

Boxed

For some reason, neat little boxes just always seem to grab my attention. If you're anything like me, then you most likely have an arsenal of little boxes sitting in various locations throughout your home, perhaps serving as bookends or vestibules for your various odds and ends. Whatever the case, wooden boxes will always be timeless additions to any style of decor, in or outdoors.

- ☐ Old cigar box
- ☐ Drill and 1/2" drill bit
- ☐ Pebbles
- ☐ Lightweight potting soil
- ☐ Pebble mix
- ☐ Succulents

HOW TO MAKE IT

1. Drill some holes near the bottom of the box on all sides.
2. Place a handful of pebbles in the bottom of the box.
3. Fill the box with a mixture of pebbles and lightweight potting mix.
4. Plant the succulents.
5. Top with pebbles.
6. Water well.

TIP: For a beachy look, top this container garden with crushed shells.

Succulent Saucepan

Don't throw out that old saucepan. Save it. Spray paint it. Fill it with soil and succulents. And there you have a brand new container succulent garden. You know what pan I'm talking about. The one that is so scratched and chipping that it is beginning to take on a color and smell of something that you're pretty sure should no longer touch food. Rather than continuing to shove it to the back of your cupboard and pretend like it doesn't exist, or just tossing it in the trash, upcycle that thing today!

WHAT YOU NEED

- ❏ Old pot
- ❏ Spray paint for metal
- ❏ Drill and 1/2" drill bit
- ❏ Lightweight potting soil
- ❏ Pebble mix
- ❏ Pebbles
- ❏ Succulents

HOW TO MAKE IT

1. Paint your pan and let it dry.
2. Drill at least ten drainage holes in the bottom and sides of the pan.
3. Line the bottom of the pan with pebbles.
4. Fill the pot about halfway with lightweight potting mix.
5. Loosen the roots on plants and place them in the soil.
6. Top with potting mix and pebbles.
7. Water well.

TIP: To get really creative, find an old-timey stove for your patio and set your succulent pot on the burner!

Bricked

Bricks offer the perfect-sized hole to display succulents of all sorts. I like to fill several and use them as table decorations if I'm having an outdoor gathering. You can even create walls and full gardens of succulent beds made from bricks. Layer and stack these easy container gardens to create a succulent sanctuary.

WHAT YOU NEED

- ❏ Bricks
- ❏ Lightweight potting mix
- ❏ Succulents
- ❏ Pebbles

HOW TO MAKE IT

1. Fill brick holes a quarter full with potting soil.
2. Loosen roots on plants and put in holes.
3. Top with potting mix and pebbles.
4. Water well.

TIP: Paint your bricks pretty colors to match your outdoor decor.

Succulent Tea Party

Ornate china teacups bring a special dainty touch to any garden. The delicate saucers provide a lovely addition and can double as a means to catch water. Mix and match saucers and cups for a unique look that will inspire recreations of childhood tea parties. So take a sip, sit back, and watch your succulents flourish.

- ❑ Teacups
- ❑ Pebbles
- ❑ Lightweight potting soil
- ❑ Succulents

HOW TO MAKE IT

1. Sprinkle some pebbles in the bottom of the teacups.
2. Fill cups a quarter full with potting mix.
3. Loosen the roots on the plants and place in the potting mix.
4. Top with potting mix and pebbles.
5. Water well.

TIP: For a fun display, plant a couple of teacups and a larger teapot together.

Rockin' Around

This little rocking chair is no bigger than four inches tall but it makes the perfect home for this darling little succulent. This project demonstrates the versatility of succulents to be at home in a wide variety of containers.

WHAT YOU NEED

- ❑ Small rocking chair
- ❑ Spray paint
- ❑ Drill
- ❑ 1/8" drill bit
- ❑ Tiny crushed rock
- ❑ Lightweight potting mix
- ❑ Pot with succulent

HOW TO MAKE IT

1. Spray paint the chair and allow it to dry.
2. Carefully drill into the seat of the chair to make a hole for the pot with the succulent.
3. Drill drainage holes in the bottom of the pot.
4. Place the pot in the chair.
5. Top the pot with tiny crushed rocks and lightweight potting mix.
6. Water well.

TIP: Place succulent in a small terracotta pot that already has a drainage hole.

Tree Funnel

Not all succulents are tiny, dainty plants that fit in the smallest of jars. Larger succulents call for something a bit more heavy duty, and this cone strainer serves that purpose well. This container already has holes built in for ease of planting and will keep you from overwatering your sensitive succulent. Hang this beauty from a tree at eye level for the full effect.

- ❏ Cone strainer
- ❏ Pebbles
- ❏ Lightweight potting soil
- ❏ Succulents

HOW TO MAKE IT

1. Mix some pebbles with potting soil and fill the strainer.
2. Plant the succulents.
3. Hang strainer from a tree.
4. Water well.

TIP: Spray paint the funnel for an added effect.

Burly and Sweet

This combination of rough wood and smooth, tiny succulents adds an interesting element to any indoor or outdoor table setting. Once you find wood that will work for this container project, you can polish it for an artistic flair. Try different types of wood or try staining it to match your other decor. Nestle the succulents into the lightweight potting soil and watch them flourish.

WHAT YOU NEED

- ❑ Wood burl (or piece of wood)
- ❑ Lightweight potting mix
- ❑ Pebbles
- ❑ Succulents

HOW TO MAKE IT

1. Test your burl first to be sure that water will drain. If not, drill some drainage holes in the sides or the bottom.
2. Fill the burl with lightweight potting soil mix and pebbles.
3. Plant the succulent.
4. Water well.

TIP: Line the burl with coconut husk or moss spilling out over the sides.

Rustic Delight

Perhaps one of the most visually appealing succulent gardens, this project closely resembles the dresser drawer project. But rather than having to sacrifice an entire dresser drawer that may still be useful elsewhere, you can instead create your own and mimic the same look with a painted handle and sides. Get creative with colors and try incorporating vibrant hues into your rustic boxes.

WHAT YOU NEED

- 1x8x16" pieces of barnwood (2 for side of box, 2 for bottom)
- 1x8x8" pieces of barnwood (2 for end pieces)
- Drill
- 1/8" drill bit
- Screws
- Decor for box
- Paint for screws
- Lightweight potting mix
- Pebbles
- Succulents

HOW TO MAKE IT

1. Screw pieces of barnwood together to make a box.
2. Attach bottom pieces.
3. Attach handle or other decor items to the box.
4. Drill drainage holes in the sides of the box.
5. Fill with a mixture of pebbles and lightweight potting mix.
6. Plant succulents.
7. Water well.

TIP: Whitewash your wood before putting it together for a cool vintage look.

PVC CONTAINER CREATIONS

Polyvinyl chloride (PVC) has traditionally been used for water and sewer lines. However, recently it has been employed in a wide variety of creative projects including tool holders, tent frames, chicken feeders, tomato cages, dog bed frames, and more.

When I discovered how fun it was to make creative industrial-looking containers for plants using PVC, I was hooked. Below, you will find nine of my favorite PVC projects that are easy to make at home with just a few tools and some creativity. These projects work for both indoors and outdoors and add a bit of "funky fun" to any space.

Note: Keep in mind that PVC pipe is suitable for non-edible plants only. Any of these projects can be made with a food safe pipe if you want to grow fruit, veggies, or herbs.

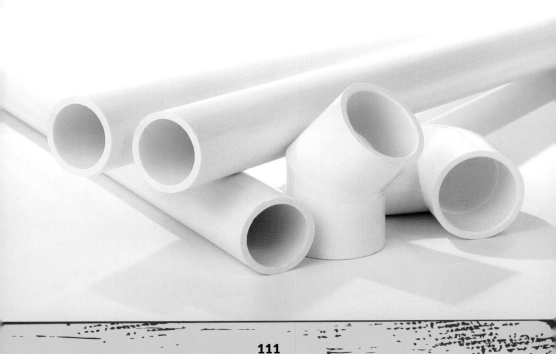

Hightower

It's amazing how a piece of plastic pipe can make your garden so interesting. Not only is it inexpensive but it is also resilient to weather and creates a great place to grow succulents or other beautiful flowers.

WHAT YOU NEED

- 4" diameter PVC pipe
- 3/4" diameter galvanized steel pipe (desired length)
- 2 nuts
- 2 washers (for the 3/4" pipe)
- End caps
- Spray paint
- Chop saw
- Drill
- 3" drill bit
- 3/4" drill bit
- Sandpaper
- Paint (for plastics)
- Measuring tape
- Pencil
- Lightweight potting mix
- Plants

HOW TO MAKE IT

1. Cut the 4" pipe to twelve inches long.

2. Find the center of the pipe and mark it. Use the 3" drill bit to make a hole in the center.

3. Attach galvanized pipe using nuts and washers.

4. Make two additional three-inch holes spaced evenly and lined up with the center hole at the ends of the pipe.

5. Put on end caps.

6. Drill drainage holes on the bottom of the 4" pipe.

7. Sand the rough edges on the planter.

8. Get creative using paint for plastics.

9. Fill the planter with lightweight potting mix and place your plants.

10. Water well.

Table T

With just a few pieces of pipe and a little bit of spray paint, you can turn
your garden into an industrial oasis. If you're going for a more modern,
streamlined look, try painting the pipe silver or copper. This T-shaped
planter allows for innumerable plant combinations to fill your garden with
vibrant color.

WHAT YOU NEED

- ☐ 3" PVC T
- ☐ 2" PVC
- ☐ Drill
- ☐ 1/8" drill bit
- ☐ Jigsaw
- ☐ PVC adhesive
- ☐ Spray paint
- ☐ Lightweight potting soil
- ☐ Pebbles
- ☐ Plants

HOW TO MAKE IT

1. Spray paint your parts and allow them to dry.

2. Drill several drainage holes in the bottom of the pipe.

3. Using a jigsaw, cut the 2" piece of PVC in half for your base.

4. Attach the base using adhesive and let it dry.

5. Add lightweight potting mix, then place plants.

6. Water well.

Piped Out

All I can say about this project is, "Wow!" What a fabulous piece of living wall art this makes. You can join the pipes in any way you wish and mount them to a wall or even a piece of painted plywood for an eye-popping display. When it's time to drain, just turn the valve!

- ❑ 1 1/2" PVC (4 ways, x2)
- ❑ 1 1/2" PVC elbows (x8)
- ❑ 2" valve
- ❑ 10' PVC 1 ½" pipe (cut whichever length you wish)
- ❑ Spray paint
- ❑ Jigsaw
- ❑ Lightweight potting soil
- ❑ Plants

HOW TO MAKE IT

1. Spray paint all the PVC pieces, then let them dry.
2. Using a jigsaw, cut the pipe into various lengths, as desired.
3. Join the pieces to create your living art.
4. Fill pieces with potting soil and plants.
5. Mount to a wall or fence.
6. Water well.

Note: If you are going to use this unique planter inside, use air plants. That way, you won't have to drain them.

Flower Boat

Forget candle boats! Whip up a flower boat to grace the flat spaces in your garden. Fill it with an easily-spread ground cover or a ground-trailing vine for a unique look. You could even try using a longer piece of PVC and make numerous holes for a more intricate display. This container garden is sure to spark conversation when used as a centerpiece for an outdoor table.

WHAT YOU NEED

- ❑ 4" PVC pipe, 32 inches long
- ❑ 4" end caps (x2)
- ❑ Jigsaw
- ❑ Drill and 1/8" drill bit
- ❑ PVC adhesive
- ❑ Spray paint
- ❑ Lightweight potting soil
- ❑ Pebbles
- ❑ Plants

HOW TO MAKE IT

1. Paint PVC pieces and allow them to dry.

2. Drill drainage holes in the bottom of the pipe.

3. Attach end caps.

4. Using a jigsaw, cut two inches off the 32" pipe.

5. Cut the above piece in half for legs.

6. Mount the legs to the pipe using adhesive, then allow it to dry.

7. Add lightweight potting mix and place plants.

8. Top with more potting mix and pebbles.

9. Water well.

"Y" Not

These sturdy little containers are extremely versatile. They can be stuck anywhere in your garden to set off green foliage with vibrant colors. Paint designs on the pipe to spruce it up even more and transfer your personality to your yard. This project is incredibly easy and can mean the difference between a drab, traditional flower bed, and a totally unique, funky backyard paradise. So "Y" not try it?

WHAT YOU NEED

- ❑ 3" PVC Y
- ❑ 2" PVC Y
- ❑ 4" PVC end caps (x2)
- ❑ Drill
- ❑ 1/8" drill bit
- ❑ PVC adhesive
- ❑ Spray paint
- ❑ Lightweight potting mix
- ❑ Pebbles
- ❑ Plants

HOW TO MAKE IT

1. Paint PVC pipe pieces, and allow them to dry.

2. Attach Y pieces to the end caps using adhesive, and allow them to dry.

3. Drill drainage holes in the sides (near the bottom) of the Y piece.

4. Add lightweight potting mix.

5. Place plants in the pipe.

6. Top with more potting mix and pebbles.

7. Water well.

Duo Delight

There's something about small, compact planters that just add so much to any yard. The details truly count, and you will be well on your way to mastering those details after crafting these mini containers. Set these planters on tables or chairs for added depth and fullness in your garden, or bring them inside to make cute indoor homes for air plants and succulents.

- ☐ 2" PVC T (x2)
- ☐ 2" PVC end cap (x4)
- ☐ Drill
- ☐ 1/8" drill bit
- ☐ Spray paint
- ☐ Lightweight potting mix
- ☐ Pebbles
- ☐ Plants

HOW TO MAKE IT

1. Paint the PVC pieces, and allow them to dry.

2. Insert end caps.

3. Drill some drainage holes on side near the bottom.

4. Add lightweight potting mix.

5. Place plants in the pipe.

6. Top with pebbles.

7. Water well.

Note: When planting cacti, wear gloves.

Flutetastic

Try mounting a few of these on various pieces of wood and staggering them along a fence. Or make several flower flutes at various heights and make a display in your garden to add a special point of interest. This plan is just a guideline—don't let it restrict your creativity with this project!

WHAT YOU NEED

- ❑ 3" PVC pipe, 32 inches
- ❑ 3" end cap
- ❑ Jigsaw
- ❑ Drill
- ❑ 1/8" drill bit
- ❑ Spray paint
- ❑ Lightweight potting mix
- ❑ Plants

HOW TO MAKE IT

1. Spray paint the PVC pipe, and allow it to dry.
2. Drill several drainage holes in the end cap.
3. Attach the end cap.
4. Using a jigsaw, cut plant holes.
5. Add lightweight potting mix.
6. Place plants in the pipe.
7. Top with more potting mix and pebbles.
8. Water well.

TIP: To hold plants in place, try adding some moss to the inside of the flute.

Simple Pleasures

If you've been inspired by this list of PVC projects for container gardening and have been busy crafting unique planters, you may have some pieces left over. For this project, you can use a variety of leftover PVC parts including end caps. This is a fantastic way to avoid waste and make adorable containers in the process. These colorful creations look great on a desk or small table as a grouping.

- ☐ 4" PVC end cap
- ☐ 3" PVC end cap
- ☐ 3" to 2" PVC reducer
- ☐ 2" PVC coupler with an end cap
- ☐ Spray paint
- ☐ Plants in pots
- ☐ Pebbles

HOW TO MAKE IT

1. Spray paint PVC pieces and allow them to dry.

2. Assemble as desired.

3. Place plants in small pots inside the PVC pipes.

4. Top with pebbles.

5. Water well.

TIME TO SHOWER YOUR CONTAINER GARDENS WITH LOVE

I hope that you have been inspired to take on some of these container garden projects or dream up some amazing garden ideas of your own. Remember, plants are living things and the more tender, loving care you give them, the more they will give back. Before any project, plan and decide what kind of plants you will use, become familiar with what the plant needs to perform well, and make it happen.

If you provide for the needs of your plants, there are no mistakes when it comes to container gardening...just loads and loads of fun, food, and beauty!

What are you waiting for? Go ahead and get planting!